Inhale...

Exhale...

Introduction

B R E A T H E

baby, B R E A T H E

is a series of empowering thoughts
that you can choose
to incorporate into every breath ...
NO MATTER WHAT.
It establishes a mindset
that will transform
your thoughts and generate
emotions and actions
of hope, power
and joy
calming and creating
a safe space for you in that moment.
Try it.... one b r e a t h
at a time

Breathe

in...

Breathe

out...

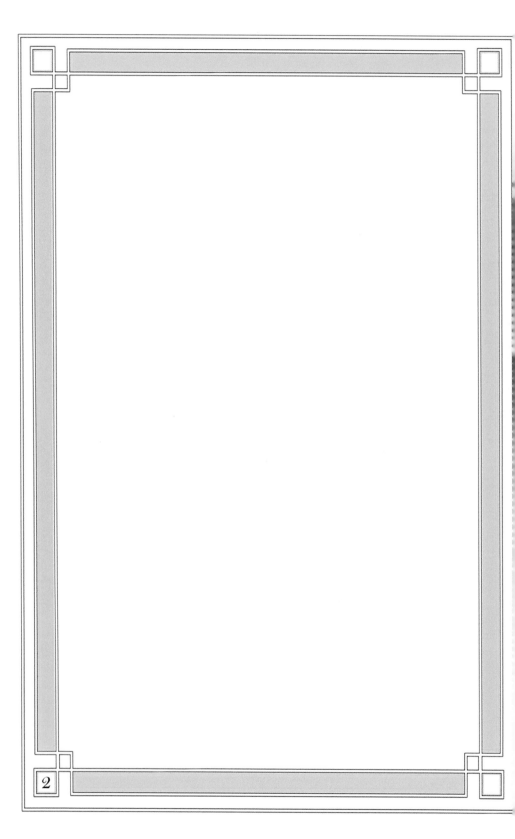

Just Breathe

by

Linda Levitt

Art by Dan Kraus

Breathe Baby, Breathe

Breathe in the beauty that
surrounds you ...

inhale the endless blessings of *life*

Release baby, Release

Free all that worries or
wounds you ...

let go of the pain, the fear, the *strife*

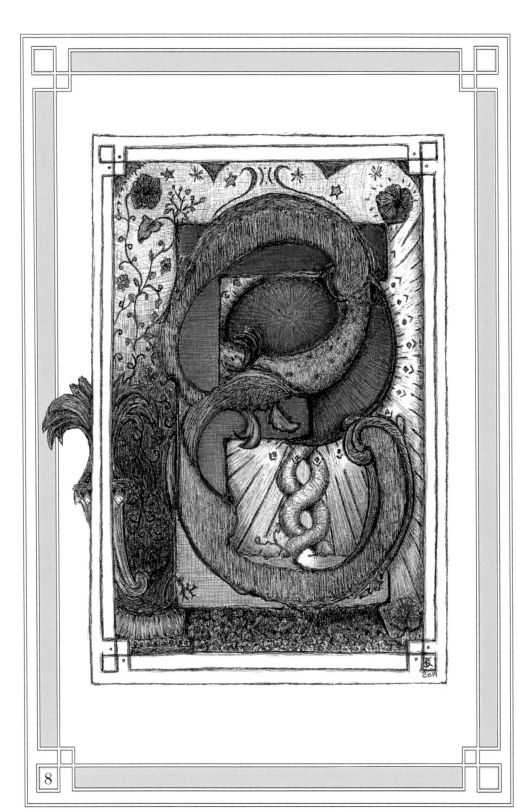

Embrace baby, Embrace

Wrap your love around
this precious moment ...

accept all that is *as it is*

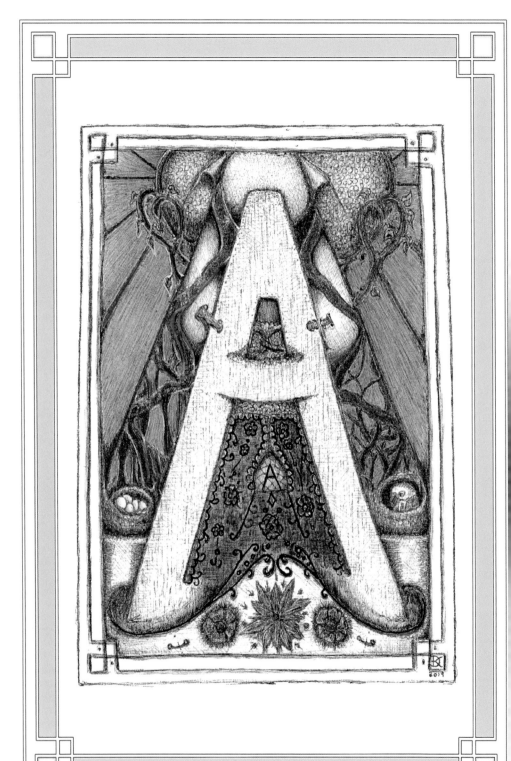

Allow baby, Allow

Compassion to flow to and
from the depths of you ...

allow yourself to *forgive*

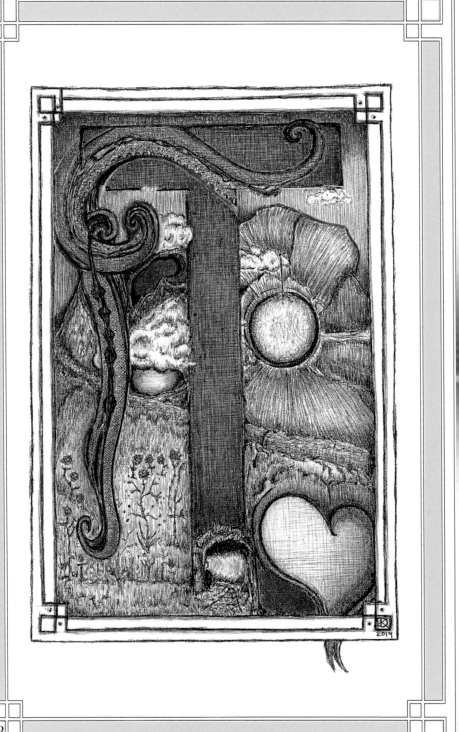

Trust baby, Trust

To be honored just as you are ...

celebrate you, your place, your *part*

Heart baby, Heart

Open your world to miracles ...

from the center of your loving *heart*

Enjoy baby, Enjoy

Choose to live **in joy** ...

breathe out what must be ***freed***

Feel the Love you need

Be the Love you need

Give the Love you need ...

Just
BREATHE

Journal

Journal

Journal

Journal

Journal

Just Breathe

by
Linda Levitt

Breathe baby, Breathe

Breathe in the beauty that surrounds you ...

inhale the endless blessings of *life*

Release baby, Release

Free all that worries or wounds you ...

let go of the pain, the fear, the *strife*

Embrace baby, Embrace

Wrap your love around this precious moment ...

accept all that is *as it is*

Allow baby, Allow

Compassion to flow to and from the depths of you ...

allow yourself to *forgive*

Trust baby, Trust

To be honored just as you are ...

celebrate you, your place, your *part*

Heart baby, Heart

Open your world to miracles ...

from the center of your loving *heart*

Enjoy baby, Enjoy

Choose to live IN JOY ...

breathe out what must be *freed*

Feel the Love you *need*

Be the Love you *need*

Give the Love you *need* ...

Just *B R E A T H E*

Illustration
by
Dan Kraus

Come Make History With Us!

join us & support

Project ⒶRT U.B.U

For The Breathe Blog & More!
visit: projectartubu.org

For More Art by Dan Kraus
visit: dankraus.art

powered by Shaibit Solutions

Manufactured by Amazon.ca
Bolton, ON

16444393R00021